Notes From Moscow

Born in 1971, Donovan Wylie was made a Nominee of Magnum Photos in 1992. *Notes From Moscow* is his third book, after the award-winning *Thirty-Two Countries* and *The Dispossessed* with Robert McLiam Wilson. He lives in London.

Notes from **Moscow**

photographs by

Donovan Wylie

PICADOR

First published 1994 by Pan Books Limited

a division of Pan Macmillan Publishers Limited
Cavaye Place, London SW10 9PG
and Basingstoke

Associated companies throughout the world

ISBN 0 330 33032 2

Introduction copyright © Tony Parker 1994
Copyright © Donovan Wylie 1994

9 8 7 6 5 4 3 2 1

A CIP catalogue record for this book is available from
the British Library

Computer typeset by Spottiswoode Ballantyne, Colchester, Essex
Printed and bound in Great Britain by BPCC Hazell Books Ltd. Member of BPCC Ltd.

For Robin and Una

Acknowledgements

Thanks to Igor Shefar; Galina Artamonova; Vladimir and Irena Stabnikov, and all at the Russian PEN Centre; Quentin Crewe; Tony Parker; Mark and Liz Johnston; Bill and Jo; Robert and MaryAnn; all at Magnum Photos; and, of course, Candida.

Preface

For this book I photographed and took notes on anything and everything which particularly struck me. As a consequence, I have ended up with a miscellaneous collage of pictures and words. But this seemed the only way. I was in Moscow during such a bizarre period of transition. No sort of order or routine in the city nor any pattern in the lives of its inhabitants, which might have informed the work and given it an obvious structure, appeared to me to exist. Now that I'm back, I think and hope that Moscow itself is theme enough.

My own day to day life was about survival — so time-consuming an activity there, that photography and writing had to be fitted into it, as opposed to the other way round. In order to maintain an integrity in what I was trying to do, I had no choice in this matter.

Some might argue that I could have lived the life of the spoilt westerner in Moscow, and gone to hard currency shops to buy my supper in a leisurely way, at the end of each day's hard photography. But to me, it was infinitely more important to live as Russians do, sharing their claustrophobic flats with them, queueing in their empty shops, and riding in their hopeless buses.

Only in this way could I fairly represent the city and its people.

Donovan Wylie

Introduction

The noble dignity of spacious avenues, the pomp and splendour of public buildings, the gigantic memorials, the sky-gazing statues motionless in stone trying to preserve their aura of being once among the truly great, the visionary concepts that never came to fruition except in the empty vistas of formal parks: and in the winter's snow and ice all of it stunned by the remorseless cold, or lying lethargic in summer almost lifeless in the stupefying heat. This is Moscow.

The brutal selfishness of horn-blasting trucks and hurtling cars, the shoving and elbowing on pavements, in the Metro, on buses, the welter and confusion of railway stations, the shouting of tired strangers at tired strangers, the carolling of laughter by friends, the unexpected passing looks, the scowls, the thoughts, the smiles. This is Moscow too.

But mostly, and overwhelmingly, it is people. At first there seems to be at least twice the maximum number that could ever be imagined to exist in the whole of the world. Whirlpooling masses swirling into crowds, pouring and flooding along streets, ebbing and flowing in groups, huddled in thousands of pairs and singles, millions at a time standing stoic in queues waiting for whatever might be at the end of the line, if and whenever it comes. Everywhere, people everywhere, every day and the next day and yesterday as well. People.

All of them, separately, individuals. And people will talk.

'Oh, my poor country,' she said softly, drawing on her cigarette and blowing its smoke out gently and watching it curl upwards, dissolving in the warm evening air. Nina Pashkova, school-teacher, forty-two: a tall, slender woman with a trim figure, big almond-shaped brown eyes and neatly cut short, curly, fair hair. Sitting on a dining chair out on the tiny balcony of her one-roomed flat high in a modern tower block on a housing estate, she stayed silent for a while before talking again.

My poor country. Do you know why I say this? I wonder if someone from another country will understand that our leaders took advantage of us for so long. Deliberately they kept us ignorant, deliberately they told us lies. Only for their own advantage. If they had not behaved like this, now we should be sure of ourselves, and happy a little and proud. They told us, well, you know what they told us, that everything in the west was bad, it was corrupt everywhere: its people had no work and no food, and it could not be avoided that soon world capitalism would collapse. So they asked of us only a few years longer, only a few more hardships and sacrifices. And then we would have our rightful place in the world, the first in the order of things. The first also in comforts, as well as in science, in art, in music, in literature, in sport, in everything. I heard them saying it when I was twelve years and when I was twenty years and when I was thirty-two.

Over and over they said this to us. But, also, that before it could happen we had to make sure we were strong and could defend ourselves against attack by our enemies. And our enemies they were everywhere, they surrounded us, they were waiting to fall on us like Hitler's Germany did – at the first moment they thought there was a weakness in our military strength. Therefore, always, we must arm ourselves and be prepared. And if it meant as a result that for a while longer there would be a shortage of food for us and few clothes and no luxury things, then our duty was to accept this and be proud of ourselves that we did.

And you know what they were doing, these men who were saying such things to us? All the time while they were telling us these lies, they were helping themselves to all the good things, all of them they could get – the comforts and the houses, the best food and clothes, everything. They were like rich men dining at a table, and sometimes they would turn their heads, like this, to look over their shoulder and tell us their lies. Every word that they said, all of it, was lies. And we, the ordinary people, were so stupid we believed them. Can you imagine that? Can you imagine now to realize how stupid we have been? I will tell you, it makes us very angry, but also it makes us sad. We are angry with them for being our misleaders, but also we are sad for ourselves that we did not have the sufficient brains to know it. To do as they said, to allow ourselves to believe them and not question them. That was terrible, that we did that. But it is true, and now we feel that we have been betrayed. There is such a word? you can say that? – we feel betrayed? Yes, well, that is how we feel.

And now I will tell you something else which I also think is the worst thing of all. It was not just by our leaders, but by ourselves we were betrayed. Because we wanted to believe what we were told, because it was more comfortable to live in that way. You understand? That is why I said my

country is a poor one, because the people in it are poor in spirit to let this happen.

And I, for myself, what was my own part in this? I will tell you, it is something of which I am very much ashamed. Because I joined in with it, I helped. I taught the children in school the same thing I was taught myself when I was twelve. I grew up and I taught it to others. I passed on the lies until I was thirty-two. I do not mean I did so deliberately, I did not know what I was saying was untruth. But I must say also I did not try to find out. A teacher has a duty to find out the truth of what she tells her children, and I did not. So, most of all, it is with myself I am angry and for myself I am sad.

I have not talked like this before. Perhaps it is the summer air. I am a left wife, but when my husband was with me, can you imagine it that we never talked? He worked, I worked, and in the evenings we read books or magazines or went sometimes to the cinema, but we never talked. For ten years we were married. Then he left me and went to live with someone else, and sometimes, you know, it comes into my mind to wonder if with the new woman also they never talk. My husband was a good man and I do not want to say things against him. But when we married I think we were too young. It is very often the case, and in time we became tired with each other. But my daughter is not like me, I am glad to say. She is eighteen and she has no thoughts of marriage, which I think is good. She is a student of engineering and so she has an ordered mind.

What do I want for her? Well, I am like every mother, I

think. I want that she should be able to make a life for herself that is good and a happy one. And I would like most of all that she should travel, and perhaps to live in other countries for a while, to see how other people are living, and not be like us, who were all the while shackled, if that is the correct word. I think it will not be long now that the time comes for her to be able to do that, to go where she wishes, and to be free. Life will be better for all young people in that way.

It has been my pleasure to talk, and I would like to say to many other people from other countries to come here and be our friends. We know they are not the monsters we were taught, and I hope they will come also, and see that neither are we.

Oleg Vadimsky, thirty-six. He said he would like to be described as a business man. Slightly portly and with receding hair, he sat in one of the plump leather-covered armchairs in his four-roomed apartment. It had bookshelves with modern novels and magazines, a colour television set, a CD player with the speakers of his quadrophonic sound system in each corner of the room, and pictures and pieces of pottery carefully displayed everywhere. His voice was brisk and his manner assured. He clasped his hands behind his head, turning it occasionally with them from side to side.

Do you do this? You should try it, it is very relaxing. Somebody showed me how to do it when I was a few weeks ago in New York. When the neck muscles are tense the effect of it spreads everywhere in the body, but when you learn how to loosen them, then the tension goes. I find it is very effective and I try to do it each evening for half an hour while I listen to soothing music such as Schumann or Brahms.

So, well, to tell you how I think things are now in our country. I would say I think they are very good. Perhaps that surprises you. Many people will say these times are bad and they will get worse, but I am not one who thinks that way. I am what is called an optimist, and it is because I am realistic: as I told you, I am a business man and it is for this reason I say these things.

Look around everywhere in our city that you go, and you will see always the same things – the holes in the main roads, that are greatly in need of repair; the clothing that people wear is all the same, as is the food and everything else too; in the shops, there is little, and the vendors on the pavement or in the subways, all that they sell is only rubbish, things like pots and pans and postcards and posters. What do they think, that people want to buy such things because there is nothing else? They do not even think if people will buy what they have to sell.

Well, I will tell you, it is my opinion this is not very good. It is not very efficient to offer something if you do not consider whether people want it or not, and you will never get very far that way. You have heard of the American firm McDonald's who have their place to sell hamburgers in Pushkin Square? Before they came, first they studied the market for ten years.

So, what I am saying is that I do not see out there only the holes, but the need for them to have repair, and I do not see only people who wear the same clothes, but the possibilities for someone who sells them others that are different. I see the opportunities that are presented, you understand? And not the ones to the market-stall seller or the man in the kiosk, but to the person who thinks on the larger scale.

When I was a younger man, shall I tell you the idea that was always here at the front of my head? It was to emigrate, to leave this country and go to another one, for example to Israel perhaps, where I would have opportunities. For many years I had this idea, and then suddenly I opened my eyes. I saw that most of all the possibilities were here. So, now I say, no, I do not want to go anywhere else, not at all, no. I want to stay here because it is where much better opportunities are. If I had gone to Israel, one thing is certain, and it is that I would have been in competition with many young men of my own age. There would be those who were born there, and those who came there before me. They would have had those advantages and I would not. So my fortunes would have relied mostly, I think, on chance.

But now? Here, today? For someone such as myself the opportunities that exist are almost without limit. And why? Because much investment of foreign money is waiting, a very great amount. It is from America, in particular, but also from Japan. It is beginning to come, but it is small compared with what it will be when the big companies see the opportunities

more and more. I am myself the exclusive agent for three such foreign companies, each in a different area of the world. One of them is in Germany and is engaged in very large building construction projects; one is American and concerns itself with retail and wholesale franchises for the selling of expensive clothing; and the third is a manufacturer of large industrial machinery for agricultural produce.

I have a good business knowledge of where investment capital is waiting, and also I have studied where openings may be found for it here. I am efficient and hard working, which many of my fellow countrymen are not. I have the capacity for careful consideration before taking decisions, and I have good ability in financial accounting. But the best of my assets, I think above all others, is my ability to communicate in English, both in its written and its spoken form. I hope you will not think I am boastful when I say that such facilities are not yet found all together in the one person here. You see, I have devoted great energy and concentration in the last three years to improving my abilities. For the whole of that period I have attended classes in the evening to study English at the polytechnic institute, and also for the same period I have had by correspondence a course from America on business studies.

I have worked very hard to be in the position I am now in. I still seek opportunities for expansion in my business agency work and it pleases me very much what is happening now, which is that companies are approaching me to represent them, when before it was I who approached them.

I am not contented yet to have gone far enough, of

course, but I think that up to now I have made a good achievement. Always I am continuing to explore new ideas and see what expansion will come here and the best direction for me to involve myself. I am, you see, not waiting now for lucky chances to happen. I feel my country is a place for great opportunities in the future and I have prepared myself for them.

Every day she was sitting on a bench at the back entrance to the block of red-brick municipal old people's flats where she lived. If the weather was warm or if it was cold she always wore the same: a thick brown coat over a dark-green woollen dress, fur-lined boots, and a tightly knotted black cloth scarf over her head. Olga Borovitsky, sixty-five: sometimes in a small group of similarly dressed women exchanging sentences now and again, other times on her own, speaking to herself her thoughts in long paragraphs. Once she had with her her sixteen-year-old grand-daughter who was learning English and gladly offered to try and act as interpreter.

My grand-daughter says you ask me to say what I think of these times. I will tell you in one sentence. Forwards, everyone says, but not me, I say back. I am an old woman and I have seen many things, and often I think other people forget. They think there is only today and tomorrow, and pay no heed to the day before. What have I seen and what have I learned? Well, yes, I will tell you that also if you wish.

I remember the Great Patriotic War, that is the first thing that there is to be said. Those who are too young to have known it, I think they cannot know very much about life. I was only a young girl for most of the time, but I remember the feelings we had. Everyone, from our leader Stalin to the smallest child in the street, we were bound closely together into one family, because we knew that to our enemy we were less than animals and every one of us was to be wiped out. You, your mother and father, your sisters and brothers, your aunts and uncles and cousins, you were not thought of as human beings. You cannot forget a thing like that, and the result of it is to strengthen the ties between you and hold you together always in a bond.

Yet I do not hate the Germans for what they did. I am too old to hate. In fact, sometimes I am almost thankful to them for it, for teaching me that bond. It may sound strange to say I am thankful, but it is true. A few years ago, when I had retired from the spinning mill where I worked all my life, to add on a little to my pension I took a position as one of the lift attendants in a big hotel in the centre of the city where tourists come. Among them there were often many Germans. They had good clothing and faces full in the cheeks because they always had plenty of food to eat. They were too young to have known the war, all of them or most, so they smiled at us and tried to be friendly, and in the city went to take photographs of the sights.

We were poor and had always lived hard lives, and at first I felt sour towards them. They had lost the war and yet they were able to come into the best of our hotels and eat good food there, which even many of the citizens of Moscow cannot do. They treated us as their servants, which we were, and thought we should be grateful to them for spending their money here as they did. They did not know the impression it created, I am sure of that. But it was a situation which was full of irony I think.

Yet I will repeat what I said: I did not hate them, I still felt so many years afterwards almost to be in their debt for having shown us what strength we have in our country. I do not think they would have understood my thoughts if I had told them what they were. They were too young, just as so many of our own people today are also, and cannot understand.

I will tell you a true story of an experience I had, to illustrate what I mean. It is a memory of my father who had been in the army in a division of tanks. He was badly injured in battle and lost the use of his arm, all the way down from his shoulder to here, so that it hung by his side. Afterwards he was sent from hospital back to his home, but he was always trying as hard as he could to make them take him back into the army again. He would not have cared however humble the work was that they gave him, all he wanted was that he could still give something to the struggle against the enemy.

One night there had been heavy bombing of Moscow from aeroplanes, and the main road a little way from our apartment had been badly damaged and blocked with wreckage. Many buildings there had been destroyed, and the people who lived in them wounded or dead. As soon as it was light enough, everyone ran to see what they could do

there to help, to rescue injured people and to try to clear a corridor through the middle of the road so that ambulances and lifting machinery could come. My father and mother and my sister and me, we were some of many hundreds, or perhaps thousands, of people who went there. We worked with our bare hands and a few shovels to begin to clear the damage.

It was very cold, everything was covered with snow, and the work was very hard. For weeks we had had barely enough food to keep ourselves alive, so we were at the limits of our strength. My father, even with his injury, set to work as though a demon had possessed him and, as a result, after some hours suddenly he collapsed and fell unconscious to the ground.

Others came to help us take him back to our home. We put him on a broken door that was lying on some stones and carried him on it, and when we got to our apartment we laid him on the ground outside, and my sister and I stayed with him while our mother went inside to prepare a bed for him. Suddenly, he opened his eyes, and when he saw my sister and I standing by the side of him he asked us in a very rough voice why we were there and not at the road. When my mother came out he asked her angrily why she had allowed us to stay there, away from where we were needed more. He said she should teach us always to do our duty to others, and not give attention only to one person alone. I could see there were tears in my mother's eyes as she sat on the ground embracing him. And then she put up her arm behind her back like this, and waved her hand at us to tell us to go away. So that is what we did. And when we returned at night, because it was too dark to see any more, our mother told us that soon after we had gone our father had died.

That was the feeling that everyone had in those days, that helping others was more important than anything. It was the most important thing of all. My father believed it with all his heart, and I am sure my mother believed it too. But that feeling has gone, and no one is like that any more. And I will tell you why. In the Great Patriotic War we did not complain that the shelves in the shops were empty and no one had enough to eat, because we knew it was the same for everyone. And so it is now, it is the same for everyone. But what do people do? They shout angrily at the politicians, and they say those in the government are responsible, and they should be thrown away.

We did not say such things in the time of Stalin. We knew we were a family, all together, and that he was the father of it. We were like his children to him, and whatever he did it was because he thought it was the best for us, as any father would. Since he died, nothing has been the same. No one could take his position because no one was like him. And I think in the rest of my life such a person will never come again.

Stanislav Torosov, student medical doctor, twenty-two. Sitting in the sunshine on a mound of grass under the trees, near the bank of the river in a park, he laughed and waved at the people passing in sightseeing boats as they chattered and took photographs and waved in return. He had shoulder-length blond hair and a beard, and wore a T-shirt with 'Pink Floyd' on it, and torn jeans.

Of the future I do not have many thoughts, you know. It is my belief it is better not to have too many ideas about tomorrow, but to wait for it to come. If it is not so good what it brings, then tomorrow after that will be not as bad perhaps, or perhaps a little better. There are many good things you can have in your life at my age, and there are many tomorrows to come. So life always feels it has excitement, you know? Some older people will say it is not responsible, to have this attitude. They say I and my friends do not regard things seriously enough. Well, it is not true. They do not know what goes on in our heads. They think we are silly people who do nothing but laugh and give ourselves enjoyment. But what they see is only the outside of us, that is all.

So many of the older people, it seems to me, they can only talk about who will solve our problems of economy in this country. They ask who will give us more food and clothes and a higher sort of living. And those who make promises that they will do that, in return the people vote for them and give them almost their lives. That is, until those who made the promises fail. Then they throw those away and choose some others instead. They, because they are political men, they give only more promises, that is all, because their interest is in power for themselves. I think it is these who are the silly people, who go on believing them.

I have an uncle who is a politician, and he says always to me he is older than me and therefore he knows more than I do and I should give him respect. I think such a man should not be listened to. There are others like him. They are twice as old as me but they do not therefore know twice as much. I do not put myself forward as a clever person to you, because I am not. But these others, the older ones, there is a word for them, I think it is 'dolt'. And as their age increases, so they become even bigger dolts.

If a man says he knows better than you what is best for you, then you will know two things about him. One is that he is a politician and so you should treat him with suspicion, and the other is that he does not know anything at all. But if a man says he does not know what is best for you, and that you should think about it for yourself, then you will know two things about him also. One is that he is not a politician trying to get power over you, and the second is that he is a good man and you should listen to him.

We have such a man at our medical school – he is a professor of surgery. But he also takes as his subject for the second part of each of his lessons some other matter as well, from a completely different area. One day he will bring in to show us for example a book with paintings by a modern artist such as Kandinsky. Or he will bring a cassette-tape of music, one time classical and another time jazz. Then again, another day a book by an old writer or a new one, and he will read to us passages from it. Whatever he brings, he tells us what he thinks of it, why it is good or why it is bad, and then we discuss it with him and with ourselves. In this way he keeps our interest always, because he gives us surprises and tries to make us think.

My girlfriend, Irena, she is also a medical student there. In the evening each day we discuss together what has been said to us by him and our other teachers, and what ideas others of the students have had. I do not know how to say this properly in English, but with Irena and I we call it our flower gathering time. It is like selecting blooms, but only the best ones, and then putting them together in a bunch so that they make a pleasing arrangement. We both like to do this very much.

Another thing we like also is to cook meals for one another and take it in turns to do it. Then one evening she chooses what we should do afterwards, and I choose the next. Perhaps we go to a theatre or a disco, or stay in our apartment to watch the television or listen to music. It is a good arrangement, I think.

And yes, perhaps one day we will get married, but we do not think the time for that is yet, because we want to make sure that we are in as many ways possible suitable for each other. By this I do not mean of course we should agree always, because we do not. Sometimes we argue with each other very fiercely: but when we do that, we do not do it in such a way that we quarrel and the situation for either of us becomes impossible to bear. We have agreed that if ever such a thing as that did happen, then it would be better for us not to continue our relationship. This is why we live together first, before marriage, to try to see if we can find out. Life is too important, I think, to waste time on unhappiness.

Well, so that is how it is for me. I am a happy person, I am a lucky person, and I think it is a good time for young ones now with so much freedom to enjoy things. I hope I have said it for you in a way you can understand.

A camera is a strange tool for a craftsman, but in some hands it is not only an example of state-of-the-art technology, it is a warm and witty communicator as well. Donovan Wylie's photographs say words and more: some take pictures that reveal others and only them, but he shows, in his choices, and choices of angles, much of himself as well.

His subject is people, and his method is seeing and looking and watching, usually but sometimes not: his work can be at one time the result of impulse, and at others of consideration, reflection, detachment of thought, or of going away and then coming back for another view. Above all, it is a response – to a taste or a touch or a sight or a sound, and from the castles he builds in the air with his feet on the ground, we see those who emerge into his sight in all their moods: stubborn and troubled, egregious and diffident, carefree and happy and blithe. Often, spotted, they turn; and he makes these moments their monuments, not frozen, like statues, but vivid and vigorous and alive.

His theme, with love, is humankind.

Tony Parker

Notes from Moscow

Blizzard, early morning, north Moscow

Chess in the park, east Moscow

Couple in the park, east Moscow

Embrace, Beloruskia station

The parting, Beloruskia station

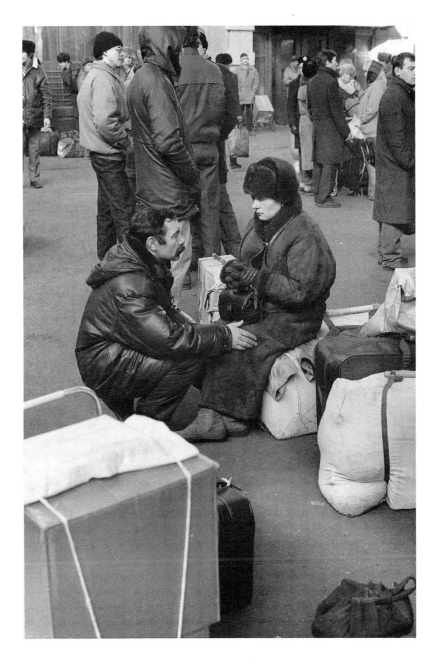

Mother and daughter, metro

Husband and wife, metro

Three generations, GUM department store

Veterans, Pushkin Square

Two stalls, market, east Moscow suburbs

Repentants, Billy Graham meeting, Olympia stadium

New arrivals, Beloruskia station

Cloakroom attendant, Central House of Writers

Gallery attendant, House of Artists

16

Army officer, McDonald's, Pushkin Square

Counter service, McDonald's, Pushkin Square

Arriving, 5 November 1992

Fly to Moscow, go into the city by taxi. So few bars, cafés, and restaurants, I'm amazed. Go to the flat where I will be staying, and meet Galina, my landlady. Her English, like my Russian, is non-existent. I had a muddled welcome. She said, 'Goodbye.'

Galina's daughter, Elena, takes me to Red Square, then leaves me there. I light a cigarette and am immediately reprimanded by a soldier. No smoking in Red Square. Amble by chance into GUM department store and go in search of underwear. Hard to find. Later I open the packet to discover my half-hour wait at the check-out counter and my $5 had bought me fifteen pairs of red, ladies' bloomers. No matter, I wear them anyway.

On the metro home the stations are poorly marked. Who knows where I am? Finally make it back at midnight.

Galina and her flat

Galina, forty, is a widowed grandmother. She is heavily built, dark-haired, and has a friendly disposition. A teacher in a nearby primary school, she earns $15 a month, which is what I give her for a week's rent.

The flat is in an area called Chelomeya in south Moscow, on the first floor of a run-down twenty-three storey tower block. Galina moved here from a small town outside the capital after her husband died in Afghanistan. The flat is so tiny that Galina has cut two holes at the bottom of the toilet door so she can straighten her legs when on the loo.

In my room I am kept warm by an old bar-heater on a rickety chair near my bed. In the corner a small statue of Lenin eyes me suspiciously as I try to sleep.

The exchange rate

I give Galina $15 which is the amount I have to live on each week. She exchanges it and gives me 3500 roubles. Two years ago, on the black market, I would have had to have given her about $440 for the same return.

Sasha

Galina introduces me to her new lover, Sasha. A quiet man, who fought in Afghanistan, he sells perfumes outside GUM. He tells me that if he could sell a bottle of scent a day, for a year, he would have enough money to take Galina to live in New York: his dream.

Does he want to have his own business, be his own boss? He doesn't remotely understand the concept of private enterprise even though he is, in effect, practising it every day, outside GUM.

News briefs

Yeltsin Reassures West He Can Block Coup Threat

London President Boris Yeltsin said on Tuesday [10 November 1992] there was a right-wing coup threat in Russia but reassured the west he could thwart it, if necessary, by adopting emergency powers.

Yeltsin's hard-hitting speech to both houses of the British parliament drove home the opposition he faces to his political and economic reform of post-Soviet Russia, where Communists and Nationalists alike are bidding to bring down his government.

In scenes a world away from Moscow, the Russian leader was treated to a full display of pageantry, first in parliament and then at a lunch with Queen Elizabeth in Buckingham Palace. The Queen accepted his invitation to visit Moscow on what would be the first trip to Russia by a British monarch since the 1917 Bolshevik Revolution.

'We must directly recognize that there are in our country forces seeking a revanchist coup,' Yeltsin told an audience of four-hundred parliamentarians and guests packed into the ornately gilded Royal Gallery of the parliament building over the Thames. But he said his government would not allow 'reaction' to triumph and pledged to press on with economic reform.

The Moscow Tribune

McDonald's

It feels too cold to get up this morning – outside it's minus twenty. Galina has breakfast waiting – raw fish. I can't eat it. When she leaves the kitchen, I wrap the fish in some old newspapers, throw the package in the bin, and go to McDonald's.

McDonald's prides itself by saying it's a rouble-only restaurant, that it's for Russians themselves. But it might as well be a hard currency restaurant because their prices are high for ordinary working people. A Big Mac, French fries, apple pie and Coke cost what it takes them to earn in three days. Because I, too, am living at that rate, I can only afford a small portion of French fries.

Eating them, I notice a deal going on next to me, a man putting a bundle of money in another man's bag. The bastards are only drinking Cokes when they could afford a hundred Big Macs. Tempted to take a picture, but know I'd be lynched if I did.

Conversation with Dmitri, medal seller, in McDonald's

I was born in 1969 so I am twenty-three, I always forget. My birthday was on 10 October, but I was unable to celebrate it because I had to go away. I went to a specialized school for English because friends of my parents said I should go into the diplomatic field. But it is very difficult without relations, acquaintances, and so on. Very, very difficult. I think everywhere now it is difficult to get anywhere without what the Russians call 'a hand'. So this field I work in now is the only one I can find where I do everything without any help, only by myself.

To be frank, I don't like this business of selling medals and coins. It's not very interesting but, you know, this is a very good way of earning money. And the most strange thing is that my colleagues are all academics. Just today I spoke to a man who's a Doctor of Science and Philosophy. But at his work he doesn't earn enough money, so he has to buy and sell and so on. Most of these people don't take it too seriously. They understand that this is only a way of earning money.

Usually I work at home but sometimes, at weekends, there are clubs where people who collect medals get together and there it's possible to buy and sell. But there is no law and I don't know if it's legal for me to buy and sell orders, because in Communist times it was impossible, and now, nobody knows. So it has to be done quietly.

On some days I have many medals, sometimes not. But I think maybe a month later, or a year later, there will be fewer and fewer because the period when sales were very good is now in the past. In Russia there are half a million Orders of Lenin, very, very many. And one Order costs more than $300, like this one for example. It's expensive because it's golden.

At the moment business is good but, as I've said, it's not very interesting for me. It doesn't fill my day. I can't sit and do nothing. If I have time I don't know what to do, well, to read, of course, but not always. So even in the morning when I get up early at eight, I really don't know what to do. The organism is ready to do something, to work, and so on. I need to find something else, something bigger, more interesting, even something more profitable. I don't know what.

I'd very much like to start my own business on a bigger scale, but it takes too much money – unless, of course, one opens a kiosk, but, again, I don't think that's very interesting. For me, what's attractive are big projects, not selling, for example, ten cars a day, but producing thousands, millions. But it's very difficult for ordinary people. All those banks, companies, which are opening everywhere now are only doing so because they have the financial backing of former ministers, the Communist party and the Mafia.

My nature is always to want too much – if making money, then a lot; if writing a book, then to be famous; if going into politics, then to become a leader. Of course it is only imagination, but this is the way I understand myself. I have a lot of energy, but I don't really know where to put it. I have given myself three more years to decide.

I can feel happy that I've achieved something without any help, because I began with zero, and now, well, I have made some zeros. Would you like another Big Mac?

Telephones and copeck coins

To ring someone from a public telephone you need a fifteen copeck coin (approximately one sixth of a penny). Because of hyper inflation they are extremely hard to find. After a whole hour of searching I come across an old woman selling them near a row of fifteen public telephones. Normally five coins cost just over a rouble. She makes me pay a hundred roubles for one – sixty-six times their actual value – and I do so because I need to make the call.

I put the almost priceless copeck in the slot of the one telephone which works, and dial. Engaged. When I replace the receiver, the copeck doesn't reappear – marvellous.

Getting the 721 bus

The temperature is minus twenty. I'm standing with about two hundred others. We're all patiently awaiting the 721 bus. Already six people have asked me for a light, and one young boy has begged me for a cigarette. I'm smoking Paparosa's because I can no longer afford my one daily Marlboro. The Russian cigarettes taste of burning rubber, but the young boy isn't complaining.

As the bus approaches everyone positions themselves exactly where they think it'll stop. There being no queue, it's each man for himself. An old woman rushes forward and falls in the snow. My guess is several metres out, so I end up with a mass of others pushing to get on. Even the thought of waiting for another bus, in these temperatures, brings on hypothermia.

I push harder. I'm hurting the person in front of me, but he doesn't say anything. The doors close. A hundred or so haven't made it. I myself am trapped, half in, half out. The bus moves off. My face is jammed up against a woman's chest. I can't breathe and everything is black. My right arm, caught between the doors, dangles outside in the freezing air. No one cares. When the bus takes a sharp corner I think I'm going to fall out. No one would care if I did.

Sasha's military uniform

Over dinner Sasha asks me if I'd like to buy his old military uniform for $30. Galina, humiliated, gives him what for. They argue for ten minutes. Sasha, while eating, resorts to reading his favourite part of the newspaper, the crime-story page. She apologizes to me, then silence.

Later she goes out and Sasha shows me the offending uniform. I buy his hat for $7. Would anybody in London be interested in buying the rest? I tell him, I doubt it.

News briefs

Rouble Falls Through 400 Level Against Dollar

Moscow (AFP) The rouble fell through the 400 point against the dollar for the first time on Tuesday in unusually light trading on the Moscow interbank currency exchange.

The rouble, which has been falling steadily since September, was marked at 403 to the dollar, compared to 399 to the dollar at the last trading session.

Volume of trading stood at 28.37 million dollars compared to 40.46 in the last trading session on Thursday.

The Moscow Times, 11 November 1992

Tourist Business to Bring in Three to Four Billion Dollars Annually, Intourist Says

Moscow (RIA) Igor Konovalov, President of Intourist holding company, expects annual revenues from tourism in Russia to rise to three to four billion dollars as opposed to the 2.5 billion it used to bring 'at best times'.

Konovalov said several hotels will be opened next year, including the old National Hotel, refurbished as a five-star establishment, and a new four-star hotel in Sokolniki.

More hotels will open in Novgorod, Pskov, Nalchik and Vladimir in 1994.

The Intourist holding company also plans to open an entertainment centre on the Arbat in 1993. The centre will have music and exhibition halls, a recording studio and a restaurant.

The Moscow Times, 11 November 1992

Record Grain Yield in Kazakhstan

Alma-Ata (RIA) A record-breaking 30 million ton yield of grain was reaped in Kazakhstan this year, exceeding the country's demand.

Baltash Tursunbayev, Kazakh Minister of Agriculture, said the excess of grain will be sold to Russia, Moldova and other CIS states. Kazakhstan plans to sell one million tons for hard currency.

As a Soviet republic, Kazakhstan used to turn in all of its grain to the central government.

The Moscow Times, 11 November 1992

Belarus Stops Selling Food for Soviet Roubles

Moscow (Reuters) Belarus halted the sale of food for old-style Soviet roubles on Tuesday to stop its goods from being bought up cheaply by outsiders, Commonwealth television said.

The National bank had introduced the move as a 'forced, temporary measure' because of a huge influx of roubles from neighbouring states which have already abandoned the currency.

The Moscow Times, 11 November 1992

President Allows Gas Pistols for People, Firearms for Farmers

Moscow (Tass) Russian President, Boris Yeltsin, has allowed Russian citizens to own gas pistols and sprays to protect themselves from crime.

He has also allowed private farmers to use hunting rifles to protect themselves against racketeers and other people who are still trying to eliminate private property in Russia.

The presidential press service announced on Tuesday that gas pistols must be registered by the police, while gas sprays need no special permission.

Private farmers can now buy, store and use hunting rifles to protect their lives, health and property, according to the decree.

This is the first time that Russian citizens have been allowed to possess weapons to protect their life and property after seventy-five years of Communist rule.

The Moscow Tribune, 11 November 1992

The Police

The chief of the police department is called Nikoli – a small man with an alarming tic in his neck and a permanent cigarette in his mouth. Scattered on his desk are photographs of wanted criminals, and of his family. There are also several dollar notes with not Lincoln's head, but Lenin's.

He asks me if I'm carrying anything with which to protect myself. Only a knife, recently bought. I don't look strong enough to use one, apparently. Moscow's a dangerous place; arms in abundance. Would I like a small pistol, a bargain at $40? I refuse, but if ever I should change my mind Nikoli tells me he's my man.

He arranges for me to go on a raid in the patrol car, a beat-up Lada. I am crushed in the back with three militia men holding rifles menacingly close to my temples. We speed over bumpy roads to a block of flats in a quiet suburb. A group of youths is arrested for theft, and possession of heroin. The militia has been after this lot for some time – they are young Mafia. A gun, several western televisions, and fifty bottles of Russian vodka in crates, all of which were destined to be distributed to the various Mafia-run kiosks around the city, are seized.

Back at the station I feel bad photographing the criminals in their cell. Later, in Nikoli's crate-filled office, a number of his colleagues have gathered to celebrate their catch. Large volumes of vodka enhance this celebration.

People selling goods in Child's World department store

Crowds of people of all ages stand next to each other outside every department store, selling cheaper, grottier versions of the goods inside. Outside Child's World they sell old toys and clothes. When they spot the store's security guards, they promptly hide their wares in their coats, and get the hell out. Now you see them, now you don't. Security know exactly what's going on but are powerless to make arrests unless they actually catch them selling something.

A young woman is selling a leather coat, and a young man is interested. After examining it closely, he decides to buy it. The woman doesn't spot the security guards. Suddenly one of them passes between her and the buyer, snatching the coat from her hands. Another frogmarches her away. While this is happening, she takes two thousand-rouble notes from her purse and gives them to the guards. They let her off the hook, but she doesn't get back the coat.

Feeling indignation on the woman's behalf I, quite loudly, but not directly, call the security men bastards.

'What did you say?' one counters in perfect English. As you can imagine, I am quite surprised, none the less so when he demands $5, the price for my western insolence.

St Petersburg or Leningrad?

Before I left for Moscow people always got at me for saying Leningrad.

'Leningrad's now called St Petersburg,' they'd say. 'You must remember that when you go to Russia. People will be extremely offended if you don't.'

Now, in Moscow, when I mention St Petersburg, people say, 'You mean Leningrad?'

'Hasn't it changed?' I ask.

'Oh, yes,' they reply, 'but nobody bothers, they all forget.'

Early morning in the park

It's early morning, I'm in the park, and I can see, quite far away, what I take to be an old man. He's jumping into a lake. What's so strange is that the entire surface, except the small part he's just jumped into, is frozen. I can't believe it. The man's bobbing up and down. Now he's getting out, drying himself in the snow, and disappearing into a tiny wooden cabin.

I don't photograph this scene because I'm too far away. But I shall return tomorrow.

The next day, I go back to the lake but can't see any old men jumping into the water. Galina tells me it's very common for people to do this, though she never has and has no plans to.

Mafia recruit having toe-nails cut,
Russian bathhouse

Empty shelves, Universal Store,
north Moscow

Meat counter, Universal Store, north Moscow

A joke at the checkout, Universal Store, north Moscow

I Love Moscow, suburban market, west Moscow

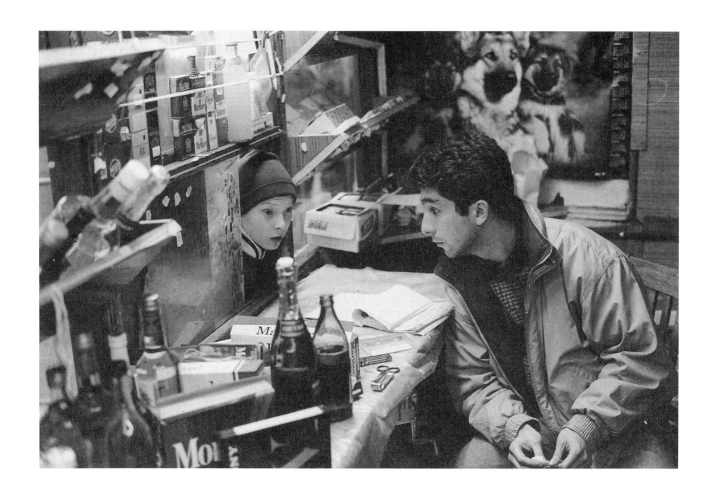

Western goods for sale, kiosk, central Moscow

Poster boy, subway stall,
central Moscow

Learning to walk

Doll seller, Child's World department
store

**Selling cats, outside
metro station**

Photographer's clown

Mafiosi playing pool, Moscow
bathhouse

Interior, Moscow bathhouse

Ice-hockey player, changing room

Spectators, ice-hockey game

Ice-hockey player, changing room

American Chilli competition

We are at dinner eating watery soup and stale bread. Galina says there's no food in the supermarkets. To add to my fury, I can hear the whining voice of a Californian journalist on the *Voice of America* radio programme. She is interviewing the winner of the American Chilli competition who boasts, 'Cooking chilli is something I do when I'm not sailing.'

Sasha wants to be next year's winner.

Lena's birthday party

I can't afford a present for Lena's twenty-third birthday, but I turn up to her party with some flowers. I am late because I had to haggle with the flower lady for twenty minutes in order to get them at a decent price.

The party's very different to what I'd expected. Everyone's formally dressed. Lena's mother has produced the largest spread I've ever seen in Moscow. She must have searched the city for days for the food. There's chicken, salami, and caviar (for which I've acquired quite a taste). Beats Galina's cooking.

There's lots of Georgian wine and vodka. In Russia, vodka isn't sipped wimpily. It is slammed, and that's all there is to it. If someone picks up their thimble-like glass, it is a sign that he or she wants to make a toast, and that all assembled are obliged to lift their glasses and swig the lot.

I am new to this practice. I keep absentmindedly taking sips as I'm chatting away, forgetting that, each time I do so, everyone assumes I'm proposing a toast and so has to slam yet another glass. Consequently, when the time comes to leave, I notice everyone has excelled themselves with their drunkenness, myself included. I fear I'm entirely responsible.

Igor

I met Igor at Lena's birthday party. He offered me a joint. Igor, twenty-four, is Jewish. His parents left Moscow in 1989, during *perestroika*, as did many Jewish people. His father worked in a factory but was always discriminated against, so eventually he walked out. Now his father works in Jerusalem in a car factory, and earns hard currency. He and his wife are both very happy.

Igor didn't want to go with them because he is studying in a Moscow film school. He has the family flat to himself. Like Galina's, it is tiny, but being full of books, and with a fridge that doesn't smell, it is infinitely more comfortable and congenial.

Igor's money comes mainly from his parents. They send him what they can which is normally around $50 a month, and sometimes food – yogurt, biscuits, herbal tea, sugar. The post is bad. They have to send it with anyone they can find in Jerusalem who is going to Moscow.

Igor supplements his income by buying and selling small items such as old watches, icons, anything he can get his hands on. It doesn't bring in much, but it all helps. As we talk, I recognize that he and I have a lot in common, particularly our great passion for photography. I sense a new friendship beginning.

Igor and the Bald People

Igor is bald. So are all his friends. They once set up a band called the Bald People. It didn't last long. These days they don't really associate with people who have hair. I have lots, so when I'm with them I feel faintly freaky. Igor believes bald people are on an intellectually higher plane than hairy people. I tell him Einstein wasn't short of a strand or two. It doesn't make any difference – he still holds the view that I'm nice but must be dim.

Grass

As far as drugs are concerned, Moscow is a boom town. All drugs coming from Asia and the southern republics pass through Moscow before heading for the major cities in the west. Consequently drugs are in abundance and can be bought at unbelievably low prices.

In the west, a pint glass filled with grass would cost hundreds of pounds. In Moscow you can buy this amount for just $3.

The penalty for being caught with $3 worth of grass is imprisonment or, alternatively, a couple of hundred dollars in the militia's back pocket.

Reggae concert

Igor and I take a metro to south Moscow. We walk through quiet, suburban streets looking for the reggae concert. It is in the evening. There are no young people around, only old ladies returning from church, so we can't ask directions.

We walk around for half an hour. Eventually we happen upon the small hall. In the cloakroom, punks, rockers – the cream of Moscow's youth culture – are already snogging each other. There is no alcohol at all. Grass is the only thing to distract everyone from their embraces. In fact, the room is so smoke-filled, you need only breathe to get stoned.

Igor's disappeared, so I've started taking some pictures. I don't get very far. Whenever I point the camera at anyone, he or she offers me a joint. Blow-backs, so much more concentrated a way of smoking them, seem to be the thing. I haven't got a hope. I head for the small concert hall itself. Run down, seedy, and pitch black, it seats about three hundred people. Some, totally out of their heads, have fallen asleep.

There are four bands, two from St Petersburg, two from Moscow – one heavy metal, one punk, the others jazz and sub-Doors – no actual reggae bands. But, because they're here to celebrate Bob Marley's birthday, they sing reggae songs. *No Woman, No Cry* translated into the heavy metal thrash, and the punk version of *Satisfy My Soul* make me feel even more out of it. The impression is not helped by the sight of the punk drummer, dressed as a Second World War German soldier, manically beating the bongo drums.

Because I'm headless, I miss a lot of good photographs. The few I do take, I must get by fluke because taking pictures has become impossible. I keep getting my settings back to front, and when I look through the viewfinder all I can see is pink elephants.

Marlboro advertisement

A dusty 1950s Marlboro cigarette advert is currently being shown on Russian TV. It shows a cowboy riding through the Grand Canyon with the exaggerated swagger of John Wayne.

'The taste of the Wild West,' is translated into Russian in a voice as flat as a Siberian plain.

Nik and his school

Around lunch time, I wander through a suburb and get talking to a youth with a guitar. Nik is sixteen, has a Teddy-boy hairstyle, and speaks good English. He studies at a nearby gymnasium (the highest grade of Russian schools). Before he leaves for his next class, I ask him if I can come along. As we go, I tell him what I'm doing in Moscow and that I'm from Belfast. He imagines Belfast to be like Beirut. I confirm that parts of the city aren't dissimilar.

Nik has a sister who works as a secretary for a western company in Moscow. She gets paid a lot more than most Russians, around $250 a month. His father died when he was five, and his mother teaches in a primary school.

Nik reveals he'd like to go to university to study law and then spend some time in another country because he's never travelled outside Russia. He believes most young Russians dream likewise. Music is his passion, especially the Police, Led Zeppelin, U2, and the Beatles. I like Nik. He is open and trusting.

His school is surrounded by trees. Nik introduces me to his English teacher, Ula. She invites me to front the class. I introduce myself. The students want to know about Belfast. Is it big? Small? Warm? Cold? Who exactly hates who? Are there tanks? How many die a day? Is George Best from Belfast? Afterwards, I follow Nik to his music class and take pictures.

I don't go back to Galina's this evening. She and Sasha have argued and aren't speaking, they need to be alone tonight. Instead, I go to Igor's, where I am now. We are drinking the bottle of Georgian wine we bought, and are admiring some Cartier-Bresson photographs.

Beggars

Every day the look of Moscow changes a little. A new hotel pops up; a new billboard appears; another litter of kiosks is hatched; there are more police on the streets; even the colours of people's clothes seems to be becoming brighter. Today it occurs to me the city is more and more filled with beggars. They aren't like beggars in England. Almost every one of them is old, very old. It is an infinitely distressing sight.

Street children are in a different category. They have the strength of youth and canniness on their side. They actually make money, sometimes a great deal. There are those among them who, with flats and riches of their own, are wealthy beyond their parents' dreams.

Going to Beloruskia station

Everybody on the metro is exhausted. Many rest their heads on strangers' shoulders. A young couple get on and sit down. Within seconds they are asleep. Resting on top of their clutched hands is a packet of cornflakes. I get off at Beloruskia metro station.

A woman is sitting on a bench. Her baby is next to her, naked. An American walks past. 'Look at that,' he says to his friend. 'Is it real?'

Further on a man is trying to kiss a woman. His face is smeared with blood. At the bottom of the long escalator to the exit, I see a couple struggling with boxes; another pair kissing; an old woman sucking on a fish bone; a Mafia-type ogling the bottle of champagne in his hand.

I take a last look before I go up. Like all Stalin's stations, it is beautiful. Over the intercom the announcer is telling people to take care on the escalator. His voice has a portentous, Stalinesque tone. All around people are laughing, their day momentarily brightened by his little joke.

Arbat

Arbat Street in the centre of Moscow has over 140 stalls, nearly all run by young people, selling military uniforms; old cameras, mostly Russian-made; *matryioshka* dolls; former USSR flags and relics; and much more.

Half way down the street a youthful photographer, who is taking pictures of tourists near an old man wearing a clown's mask, asks a passer-by the time. He tells the old man he can go for lunch. I follow him. He doesn't shed his mask, but turns into an alley, through an untidy courtyard, and down some steps leading to a basement. He sits on the bottom step, out of view, and finally takes off the mask and eats some bread. His face is extravagantly scarred. He looks irredeemably sad.

After half an hour he puts on his mask again and emerges from his hide-out. He spots me for the first time as I take a picture of him walking back to Arbat Street. Trying to avoid my lens, he lowers his head. The tourist photographer shouts at him for being late but he doesn't answer back. Instead he takes off the mask, places it on the ground, and wanders away.

Who needs yesterday's newspapers?

Answer: In Moscow, everybody. The Russians seem to come up with more and more ingenious ways of utilizing this humble resource. Every day I am amazed by discovering yet another.

1. Bundles of newspapers are kept in Galina's toilet. She uses them not only as toilet roll but also as an air freshener. By burning bits of them with a match, all bad smells are instantly eliminated.
2. Galina scrubs her windows with old papers each morning, to scrape away the ice.
3. I have two pairs of shoes. One, a pair of vast DM boots, falling apart, that I wear when travelling. At two sizes too big, they're perfect for Moscow because they can accommodate any number of thick socks. The others are old-fashioned leather shoes, respectable. I want to wear them when I get back to London, to feel smart again.

I ask Sasha if he has any shoe polish. He disappears, only to return minutes later with a bundle of old newspapers with which he begins to scrub the scuffed toes. This is shoe cleaner, Russian-style. It works perfectly.

Galina tells me how much
the agency pays her

Galina tells me that Globus, the western agency with which I arranged my accommodation, pay her a desultory $1 a day, that's $60 for my two-month stay with her.

This is a risible sum considering I paid Globus a total of £1200, or $1800. When I tell Galina this, she breaks down in tears. She feels, naturally enough, exploited. I am surprised that Sasha isn't surprised.

Galina politely asks if I could give her some extra money. I manage to scrape together $200, which I've been keeping aside for my ticket from London to Belfast. Now I am completely broke. Nevertheless Galina, for once, is smiling. And Sasha is back on top form.

Arrive back one night to find no fewer than three new wardrobes in the flat. They are so big there's hardly room to move. They cost $10 each. Galina paid for them out of the $200. I ask her what she'll put in them, because she hasn't exactly got many clothes. Newspapers, she tells me sharply. Of course. More than anything, Sasha says, the wardrobes make the place look smart.

Leaving

Saying goodbye to Galina isn't easy. She serves my last dish – watery soup with fried pasta shells – and tells me how much she'll miss me. I don't say much, except that she mustn't worry about her daughter's divorce. 'It's not your problem,' I tell her, and she agrees.

Her face is like that of a child whose toy has been confiscated. Galina begins to cry. I hug her, then leave.

Outside, the surrounding tower blocks are obscured by heavy snow. As I walk to the bus for the last time, I look back to see Galina waving to me. If I allow myself to feel sad, I'll crumble.

One more night

My flight's been cancelled because of the ferocious blizzard. British Airways has put me up in an extremely posh hotel near the airport called Novotel. I'm pretty pissed off about this as I've absolutely no money left so can't get any cigarettes. I should be relishing the luxury. Instead I'm just frustrated.

In the restaurant over chicken and potato salad (compliments of B.A.), I meet an English doctor, John. He's been in Moscow with a whole team of people who've been sent to advise and pass on their expertise to those working in the Russian health service. He tells me it's been hugely rewarding. Russians are keen to learn, and to work hard. He doesn't particularly want to return to London.

I also meet James, a young man from Burger King in Glasgow. He's been in the city giving lessons in marketing to Russian businessmen. He visited several factories and shops.

He said, 'When I tried to tell them, "The customer is always right," they laughed at me, and said, "The customer's always drunk."'

Aeroflot

British Airways chicken out of flying this morning. They say the blizzard's too strong. Passengers are given the choice of another night in Novotel, or flying a few hours later with Aeroflot. Seventy-five per cent opted for the former. Not me. I wouldn't like to pass up the chance to risk flying with the world's dodgiest airline.

The confidence is not inspired by the take-off. The plane heaves and rattles spectacularly. When we're airborne at last, I open the bag Galina's given me. In it she's put a loaf of bread, and a note. The man at my side translates it for me. It says, 'Russia is waiting for you.'

Returning, 4 January 1993

I'm on the train, passing through somewhere in Germany, heading for Moscow once again. I'm excited at the prospect of taking more photographs there, staying with Igor, and seeing all my friends.

This time I'm well prepared. Normally a light traveller, I am now weighed down with bags of sugar, jars of coffee, tins of Heinz beans, pots of M&S houmous, and a protein drink supplied by the doctor called Build-ups. They won't last for long, but will get me through the period of re-adjustment.

My first experience of a Moscow supermarket

Russian supermarkets are called 'Universal Stores', and are about as universal as golden samovars. Outside the one I go to, near Igor's apartment, some drunk men are having an argument. Close to them a check-out girl is taking a cigarette break with her boyfriend. Inside the place is packed with people, spending hours, shuffling around, trying to find enough food to piece a meal together.

I, like everybody else, fail to get sugar, butter, milk, or bread. Quite simply, there is none. So I head for a small hatch which sells pizza. When I ask for a slice, a middle-aged man begins to make it. A cigarette dangles precariously from his lips, and some ash falls onto the dough. He flicks it off and, wholly unconcerned, carries on with the preparation. I pay 58 roubles. It tastes of filthy, cheap cooking oil. Such is my hunger, I eat it anyway.

Close to the pizza hatch, children are queueing to buy popcorn. 'The American Taste' is proudly printed on the bags. Each one costs 100 roubles (about 40 cents).

At the tills, boyfriends keep the check-out girls entertained. The queues are long, the people in them all poor and morose. Some read, some chat dejectedly as they wait, yet others look just cross.

I show the check-out girl the figure 89 which I've written on my hand because I can't say it in Russian. She thinks I'm deaf. I then give her the money and she gives me a receipt which I take to the counter selling biscuits at 89 roubles a packet, and give it to the fat biscuit saleswoman. She chats to her colleague for a full ten minutes before deigning to hand them over. Shopping for even the simplest things is rendered a gruelling business.

The busiest part of the supermarket, and the most crowded, is the cosmetic counter. The blonde woman behind it is applying her mascara in a leisurely fashion while at least twenty customers patiently await her assistance. As one contemplates buying some lipstick, a fight breaks out over at the empty bread counter.

The woman behind the counter in the liquor section is asleep. I have to wake her in order to buy a bottle of Pepsi. As I drink it, the man next to me collapses. A young militia man arrives. We lift the sick man onto a bench. When he comes round, I offer him a swig of my Pepsi, and he gulps the lot in one go.

The militia man hasn't been able to get an ambulance, so he and I go outside to try and flag one down. We stand on opposite sides of the road in the freezing cold. When we return in vain to the supermarket an hour and a half later, we find the man happily sitting up, and flirting with all the check-out girls. The militia man remonstrates with him, but is told, much to his annoyance, to fuck off.

The knife-sharpener

Igor and I finally get round to going to Tinshkaya market. The blizzard resembles one found in a bad Hollywood horror movie where the designer's been over-enthusiastic with his special effects. The cold grips my balls so they ache. Few have ventured out – few have the same foolhardy optimism as ourselves.

Those who have are selling empty bottles, dead light-bulbs, old car parts, tatty shoes, all useless things. Igor tells me to be patient, he wants to find something he can buy now, sell later. I stumble behind him. The winds are too strong for me to take pictures, and my fingers too numb.

Two old men are selling what they pass off as an electric knife-sharpener, but which is really a small motorized stone wheel. Igor's eyes instantly fall upon it. 'How much?' he asks.

The answer comes back – 2000 roubles (about $8). The old men, drinking vodka, do a hard sell, pointing out the machine's finer features. Igor tells me he can get a better deal if he holds them in suspense a bit and comes back later. We wander off.

We enter a nearby café selling tasteless sausages and coffee. The middle-aged woman behind the counter is very frisky, attractive. As she moves around, she gives everyone the eye and cracks jokes at which only I laugh.

Heading back to the old men, I notice the sun breaking through and creating a strange light which I try to capture, but cannot. Igor looks at the sharpener again and asks to see it in action. Problem: no electric sockets to be found in a blizzard. With the scraggly men, we head back to the café where the chirpy woman's happy to let us test it. It works well, and Igor produces the cash. As he does so the woman asks what it is, then offers to buy it. The old men are overwhelmed by their good fortune – two potential customers! The haggling begins.

The woman offers 3500 roubles. Igor tips it to 4000, but can go no further. Then the woman adds two large free meals to her original bid, and the men can't resist. The promise of her sausages proves too great an attraction, and Igor loses his sharpener.

The criminal morgue

I'm not particularly keen about going to the criminal morgue. Dead bodies are not that interesting in themselves and I am not crazy about them. The stuff that makes people intriguing to photograph is gone from a corpse – a living person is much more exciting. Those ubiquitous, dead images of war victims are as dehumanizing as war itself. Great images are rarely the bloody ones.

My friend, Felix, makes the arrangements. He knows people at the morgue, having worked there himself at one time. Generally, the staff are young men and girls in their late teens or early twenties. The money is pretty good, perhaps the equivalent of $35 a month.

Our bus runs through the quiet streets to a tree-filled suburb. The characterless nature of the morgue building is emphasized by the fact it has no windows. Felix's friend is an amiable, blond lad of about twenty, who shakes our hands in welcome. He wears a blood-stained, rubber apron and has the air of an apprentice butcher. He eyes my camera and announces that pictures are out of the question, though he's happy to show us round.

In the office hanging with posters of bedraggled, naked women, the other morgue attendants sit around with girls on their laps, smoking and drinking vodka. They press us to join in their drinking and it would plainly be rude to refuse. A clapped-out TV burbles out a Russian soap and something boils on a small gas-ring. This I feel I can refuse without offence.

By the time we go into the mortuary, we feel drunkish. One of the morgue attendants sets caps of vodka bottles on

Ice-cream

the top of upright coffins and begins shooting at them with an air rifle. He offers me the rifle and I take a shot, but can't aim well.

He leads us into the main room of the morgue. Dozens of corpses in every stage of decay lie strewn, haphazard, across the floor. It is hard not to vomit at the stench. The young attendant with the rifle diverts his attention from bottle caps to more exhilarating targets in the form of the swarming rats. He manages to kill several.

Old men keep bringing in more bodies. They throw them down on the ground without feeling. I snatch a picture.

Every day is so cold, never above minus fourteen. In the circumstances, I find it extraordinary that so many people on the streets can be seen eating ice-cream. Cones are for sale on every street corner, at 28 roubles each. This is dirt cheap, but their popularity in these temperatures still makes no sense to me.

A friend of Igor's says, just as hot tea in India is supposed to keep people cool, so ice-cream in Russia keeps people warm. I find this explanation improbable, and remain completely baffled.

Price of metro and bus tickets increases

A journey on the metro no longer costs one rouble, and probably never will again. It is now three roubles. Bus fares have also increased from one rouble per journey to four roubles. Fines for not paying have gone up from 50 roubles to 250 roubles (about 20 cents to $1).

Metro tickets have increased a further three roubles so now it costs six roubles a journey. Metro coins have also changed. The once copper coins have been replaced by transparent green ones.

Sausages

Everywhere I've been today, I've seen people queueing beside lorries stuffed with sausages. Where did all the sausages come from? When I return to the flat, Igor tells me he too has seen lorry-loads of the things all over the city. He believes they have arrived courtesy of foreign aid, presumably from Germany, because they're all frankfurters. We shout at each other when we discover we've both failed to buy any.

We decide immediately to go to the Universal Store, and arrive to find hundreds of others have had the same idea. Small fights break out as people try to jump the frankfurter queue. When our turn comes, we buy 150, at about $20 the lot.

Once home, we find we can fit just thirty of them into our modest fridge. Thus, we strike a deal with our neighbours. For every ten sausages one of them stores for us, we give them two. A week or so passes, and a number of our sausages mysteriously disappear from our neighbours' fridges. Several say their dogs have eaten them, while others claim we never gave them any in the first place. We are seventy-six sausages down.

Gorbachev, speech to US
businessmen, American Press Centre

Fatherland Day, Communist march

In celebration of Communism, Manezh Square

The old guard, Manezh Square

The new generation, young Yeltsin supporter, Manezh Square

Hardliner, near Red Square

Reformers, Manezh Square

Stalin for sale, Tinshkaya market

New Communist, Red Square

Stroke victim, near Red Square

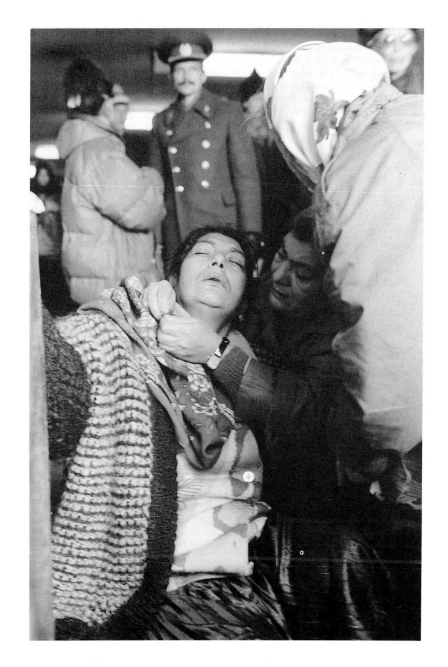

Patient receiving medicine, District Hospital

70

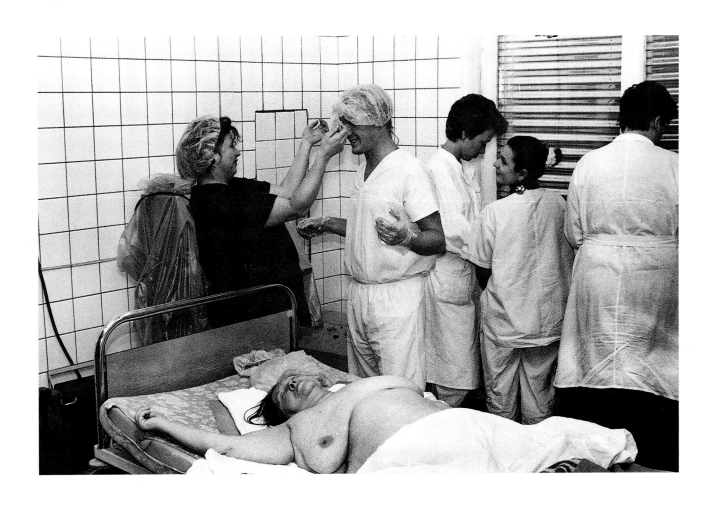

In preparation, District Hospital

Nurses at rest, District Hospital

Criminal morgue

Demi and the hospital

Demi, a young doctor, answers a telephone, looks concerned, nods and hangs up. 'Do you want to see a situation?' he asks me.

We run down a long corridor and go into a dark ward. A very ill patient, heavily built and in her fifties, is groaning loudly. Demi feels her pulse and puts his head to her heart. A woman in the next bed wakes up and asks questions. Demi doesn't reply, keeps his head to the sick woman's chest. Other patients begin to wake, too, and ask me questions. I don't speak Russian, I tell them, feeling embarrassed and stupid.

I help Demi push the heavy bed to the recovery room, an awkward task. I notice medicine in wine bottles, a machine which is cumbersome and rusty. The paltry amount of equipment shocks me. Young nurses appear in seeming high spirits. One puts on the radio. Madonna singing *Vogue*. Another dances.

A large syringe is being prepared. Demi insists I take pictures, then carefully injects the woman's back, towards her right lung. Although unconscious, she lets out a howl. Then something terrible happens: the syringe breaks inside her. Demi curses noisily and a nurse turns the radio down. Another syringe is prepared as Demi delicately cuts around the wound. He grasps the tip of the thick needle and pulls it out. A nurse hands him the new syringe. He squirts a little of its contents into the air, then reinserts it. The woman groans again when it's removed.

Demi and I return to the office. He makes tea, smokes incessantly, and tells me how much he enjoys being a doctor. His main work is performing minor operations though more often than not they are emergency ones.

Pay is poor – $15 a month – so in his spare time he also publishes crime novels, though this is more of a hobby. His work as a mechanic, repairing cars, is the most lucrative of his occupations. He once spent time in an American hospital. He couldn't believe the contrast with Russian ones. Toilets worked, wards were clean, there were endless supplies of medicine and equipment. He hopes to return. It was every doctor's dream.

He feels that the managerial control of Russian hospitals, including his own, should be improved. He is bitter that some doctors and nurses charge patients for the most basic of needs, including clean sheets.

Somebody knocks at the door, a patient. Outside a rough-looking woman is lying on the floor. Demi manoeuvres her into a recovery position and thanks the patient for alerting him to her. I take pictures. The woman is drunk but Demi doesn't seem concerned about her state of health. She has wandered in from the streets. He explains that this is a common problem which only started about a year ago. Hospitals are feeling the effects of economic collapse; people are dropping like flies.

Demi is in a difficult situation. The woman isn't sick so he can't admit her even though it's minus twenty outside. The hospital is already short of beds. He has no choice but to call the hospital militia who come to take her away. I admire Demi for his brave decision. The woman is struggling with the two militia men. I feel for her. After taking a few more photographs, I return to the office and fall asleep.

Clinging to life

What is so remarkable about the Muscovites is their tolerance of life. People are living in a manner which owes more to the eighteenth century than the twentieth, yet they don't try to escape life itself. The very hardship they endure seems to have bestowed upon them a singular, admirable determination to live through and survive the transition, no matter how long it takes.

Today there is literally no food in the shops. Ravenous and weak, I whinge on to Igor, but he seems remarkably resilient, nonchalant even. He is too excited about the future, too keen to know how things are going to turn out for him and his country, to notice basic deprivation. It seems not to touch him anything like as much as it does me. For him, compared to the big things, it is a trifle.

I am reminded of a story I heard about a very old Russian lady called Irena. She was sixteen at the time of the Revolution, and in the top form at her school. All the teachers went away, so her year were in charge. They loved it. Tickets to the ballet were freely available. She said that of course they were hungry, but that they didn't feel it. They were all too excited about living during this historic period, and about what on earth was going to happen, to give any regard to their stomachs.

'Cruel Russians'

Igor shows me a piece in today's *Pravda* which would seem to belie what I said in yesterday's journal entry.

About 2000 Russian children and adolescents have committed suicide in the past year, mostly victims of cruelty in the home, a doctor said in an interview.

Tamara Safonova also said that investigators in the former Soviet Union had uncovered more than 1500 cases in the past five years of mothers killing their own new-born babies. Child abuse in Russia was an extremely grave problem that was aggravated by the harsh social and economic climate, she said.

Despite these statistics, I still believe that there is an amazing resilience among the Russian people.

Igor and his bugs

Igor is convinced he's infested with bugs. He thinks he has caught them from travelling on the buses and the metro. He knows who the culprits are – namely, the Caucasus mountain people who arrive in Moscow daily, in their droves. He doesn't trust them, what with their primitive ways and unwashed looks. To him they are the 'Dirty People'.

Igor has taken to scratching himself in a major way. He comes in at night, jabbering all the while, unaware that while he does so, he is scratching his thigh with one hand, his chest with the other – violently. As he wanders about the room, he lets his trousers drop to his ankles, lifts his shirt, lets out a sigh, and just keeps on scratching. I am reminded of a baboon.

Elaborate plans are laid to get his parents to send the very cream he needs from Israel. Doctors in Moscow haven't a clue, and prescribe only useless stuff. The dispatch from Jerusalem duly arrives. Igor proclaims the contents to be just the thing. But I wonder, for his scratching, and his complaining, persist.

I arrive home every night to find him, sitting naked, poring over a pail of boiling water. In it, every piece of clothing from his wardrobe, including his tie, is bubbling away. In a separate pot even his shoes are getting similar treatment. He's hoping to kill all bugs.

One morning I'm woken by Igor. His face, looming over me, has an expression of extravagant anxiety.

'I slept with Gallia last night,' he says gloomily.

Igor is hesitant about sleeping with girls (though it isn't AIDS which prompts this hesitancy), and I know Gallia to be very attractive. For these reasons, though still half asleep, I applaud his success.

'Yes, but there's a problem,' he says. 'The bugs.'

'What d'you mean?'

'Well, she might get them now. I've bugged her.'

I laugh.

'Seriously. The bugs. What'll I do?'

'Forget about it,' I say. 'She'll be fine. Go back to bed. Make love again.'

He wobbles off, scratching.

Later, when I get up, Gallia's already left. I find Igor in the kitchen, desperately worried. Unable to bear the suspense any longer, he calls her to see how she is. He dares not ask her directly if she's itchy, but instead asks after her health in general.

'How did she sound?' I ask when he puts down the phone.

'Her voice was odd. I think she may be sick.'

I tell him I doubt it.

The next day Gallia comes for supper. During the course of the evening she happens, once, nonchalantly, to scratch her knee, but not so as I notice. Igor does though. He takes me aside and gravely wonders whether he should give her some of his Jerusalem cream. I laugh. Still, he offers it to her. She then laughs till she cries. Igor, embarrassed, is also faintly relieved.

London, May 1993

To this day, Igor continues to scratch, but he and Gallia are still together.

I have started to scratch now too. I am a bit ashamed to admit to my girlfriend, Candida, that I might have caught Igor's bugs . . . Her turn to laugh. There is a disease, she tells me, of a psychiatric nature. It is called *delusory parasitosis*.

The itching stops overnight.

News brief

Warring Factions
Take Battle to the Airwaves

Russia's warring executive and legislative powers have tussled over an impending constitutional referendum in round tables and face-to-face meetings, but now they are taking their differences to a battle for the airwaves.

Only one day after the head of Russia's largest television network turned in his resignation to protest over what he called the absolute power of the Democrats, hardline leaders in parliament moved to bring the broadcast media under their control.

In a parliamentary hearing called on Tuesday morning to discuss a draft law on the broadcast media, deputies urged that parliament assume control of the programming and appointments of executives of the Ostankino Television and Radio Company, the former Soviet Union's main network.

'It's very sad, but if such a law is adopted, then the mass media will be at the centre of this political battle,' said Kirill Ignatiyev, a member of the Liberal Democratic Choice bloc of deputies who attended the hearing.

Such a law would allow the parliament to set the political orientation of Channel 1, which is now financed and controlled by the federal government.

While Russia has had a general press law since the

Igor and the hi-fi

end of 1991, this would be the country's first legislation passed specifically to regulate the broadcast media.

The Moscow Times

Igor buys a hi-fi for $30. It has no speakers, he has no tapes. But it's a very good hi-fi. It's a Phillips, he enthuses.

I pay for it, a present. In return he gives me three 1960s Czech photography magazines, and a postcard of a voluptuous Parisian nude. They are beautiful.

District disco

The district disco near Igor's is a bit like a youth club, only it starts at 11 pm and ends at 5 am. I arrive at ten-thirty. The twenty-year-old doorman introduces himself as Demi while I'm paying for tickets, and offers me a pretty young girl for 'a little money'. I refuse.

Inside, the division between the two types of young people who go there is marked. On the left side of the room is the group of typical teenagers, dancing, drinking, simply having a good time. One boy looks on wistfully as a couple kiss. On the right is the rough lot, all pissed. Many are arm-wrestling for money, or getting into scuffles. All of them are looking aggressive. Of course, it is these ones I want to photograph, and it is these ones who are going to give me a hard time for doing so. At first they push me away, but I manage to charm one.

Soon an ugly middle-aged man with a briefcase joins us. The arm-wrestling stops immediately, and he is greeted warmly. I realize he's a Mafia member coming to check up on his young apprentices. A youth asks if I can take a picture of them all together.

After doing so the ugly man asks me a question. I tell him I'd be happy to send him a print. He then hits me so hard on the nose that I fall to the ground. Demi is frightened of rescuing me, but does so eventually, and takes me to a back room. My mistake had been not to give the ugly man the film there and then. The Mafia don't wait.

I switched the film, and gave Demi an unexposed one to give the man instead. Serve him right for his impatience.

Millionaire's day out

Mark, twenty-four, from Belfast, is a typical westerner on the make in Moscow. He sells *dachas* to rich, mainly American, businessmen, and proposes not to leave Russia till he's earned £100,000. He asks me to accompany him and a treasure trove of his potential clients on a day trip to see an ice-hockey match, and to relax at an exclusive country club outside the city.

I join their bus near the posh Metropole hotel. It is a posh bus with heating, velour seats, televisions, and a toilet at the back. Smart men with sharp suits, Rolex watches, and flushed complexions, take up all available seats. I am late and am forced to stand, the only one who has to do so. With my bedraggled hair and jaded clothes, I stick out like the proverbial spare prick at a wedding.

The country club, in a forest, is basic. We are greeted by Jim Anderson who's been wheeling and dealing in Russia since the days of Brezhnev. He has a gold mine in Kazakhstan, and hands us all blue baseball caps emblazoned with its name, Californian Creek.

We all head for the ice-rink in a nearby run-down suburb, and arrive just before half-time. We stand amongst the supporters and the millionaires eat their packed lunches – tactless smoked salmon sandwiches which prompt looks of envy from the Russians.

I go off to photograph the players in their changing room, and some spectators. I meet up with the others again, after the match is over. I don't think the millionaires enjoyed it. They were cold and bored and wanted to get back to the club. Jim Anderson and Mark had perhaps misjudged their notion of pleasurable corporate entertainment.

When we return to the club, they immediately head for the saunas. I find myself in one with Jim's wife. Managing to look brassy, even in only a bikini, she flirts with me, massively. I suggest she should take off her knuckle-duster of a ring because it might scorch her fingers in the heat. She declines, saying she's scared of losing it, and exploits the opportunity to let me know it cost $40,000.

Afterwards, in the rest-room, a television, with the sound down, is showing pictures of starving children in Somalia.

'Oh,' pipes up Jim's wife, 'isn't it just awful what's happening in Madagascar!'

The episode depresses me immeasurably, and my mood is not enhanced by Jim's parting shot – 'I've been meaning to ask you, Donovan,' he asks as we're about to leave. 'Is the IRA Catholic or Protestant?'

Billboards

Hundreds of modern, back-lit billboards advertising western products are popping up all over the centre.

They are a complete nonsense to ordinary Muscovites, who cannot begin to afford a single one of the products.

Snickers bar

Probably the most visible sign of free-market growth in Moscow is the increasing number of kiosks around the city. The centre itself is coming down with them. The goods they sell are mostly cigarettes and Snickers bars.

What with food shortages, the Snickers bar has become a sort of national food. Everywhere you go, you can see signs advertising them. Old women sell dozens by the hour outside metro stations. People on buses can be seen, laden with boxes of the things, as they head for some spot from which to sell them.

When I arrived in Moscow a Snickers bar cost under 100 roubles (then about forty-two cents), an attractive enough price for everyone. Just when everyone had become hopelessly and completely addicted to them – brilliant marketing ploy – the price went up, over double. I'm currently on five a day. It beats queueing.

Taxi drivers

Taxi drivers can spot a westerner a mile off. Quite apart from most westerners' inability to speak Russian, or their giveaway foreign accent if they do, there is the matter of their clothes. Sartorially speaking, Russians are not bright. Grey, black, and brown is what they all wear. If someone is in red, or yellow, or green, for example, it's an almost dead-cert they're a stranger to these parts and so, in taxi drivers' eyes at least, easy prey.

My hair is shoulder length and therefore, to the Russian way of thinking, rather decadent. This, together with my old jeans, means I haven't a hope of passing myself off as a Muscovite.

When I arrived in the city, I'd tell taxi drivers where I wanted to go, and pay for it, with grossly over-inflated fares. I've since wised up. Now I hand them notes with addresses of my destination and, gesturing with my hands to my ears, pretend to be deaf. These days taxi drivers not only charge me the right fare, some even charge below the odds.

Lunch break, textile factory

Chat, textile factory

Workers, textile factory

End of the day, textile factory

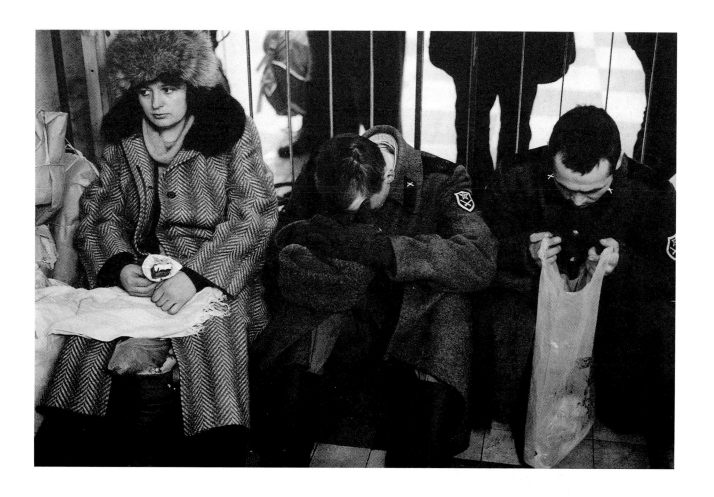

Waiting room, Beloruskia station

Young pianist,
Moscow Music Academy

Opera lessons, Moscow Music Academy

Military band, bus, Moscow

90

Young rocker, suburban park, south Moscow

Backgammon and memorabilia, Arbat Street

Street gang drunk on metro

Arm-wrestling at the district disco

Circus entertainers

Child, Beloruskia station

Young hippy, apartment,
central Moscow

Birthday party, north Moscow

Ambulance

Because so many buses have broken down due to over-use, the last bus time has been put back from 1.30 am to 11.30 pm. Igor and I have failed to hear of the new timetable, and stand waiting for the bus to take us the two miles home. It's midnight and, at minus eighteen, far too cold to walk. There is nobody else around, and we wait for an hour before a passer-by tells us we've missed the last bus. We don't have a rouble between us and, unsure of what's going on, decide to hitch.

The first driver who stops says he'll take us home for the extortionate sum of $3. Igor is incensed. There was a time, he says, when people were happy to give lifts for nothing. Eight more cars stop, all demanding money. We have to refuse. A short time later, Igor is excited by the sight of an ambulance approaching. Ambulances are normally driven by young students happy to give lifts if there isn't an emergency.

The ambulance stops. There is a man in the back making noises like the death rattle. It is clear he should get to the nearest hospital, fast. Even so, the ambulance driver says he'll take Igor and me home – price $5. Igor is shocked to the core, and abuses the callous driver. We end up walking home after all.

Night Flight nightclub

Moscow has few nightclubs. A year ago it had none. Those which do now exist are expensive, around $20 just to get in, so few ordinary Russians can go. The people who do are mainly young western businessmen.

My camera is confiscated before I even get through the door of Night Flight. I ask the smartly dressed doorman why I'm not allowed to take pictures inside. House rules, he tells me abruptly.

I persist. 'This is ridiculous. What've you got to hide?'

'Diplomats,' he says reluctantly, and I go in minus camera.

The place is very small and very dark, with a dance-floor the size of a rouble, and more prostitutes per square inch than commuters on a Moscow bus. They sit in groups drinking beer and chatting amongst themselves while greasy men grope their breasts. Images are crying out to be recorded, but I can take pictures only in my head.

I am chatted up by three prostitutes, all attractive. The first, Natasha, is in her late teens and wears conspicuous earrings, miniature chandeliers.

'Fuck me for $200, OK,' is her opening line. I thank her for her interest but tell her I'm poor.

'A blow-job for $50 then,' she says. I tell her I'm very poor, and she leaves.

The second, Ula, is slightly older than Natasha and less attractive. She studies English at the state university, her mother is a dress-maker (in fact it was she who made the purple dress Ula has on now) and she 'very much like' to sleep with me. Asked the price, she answers, '$150', with excruciating shame, then asks for a light, and tells me how much she hates her job.

Ulga, the last, has large breasts and is the most persistent. She puts her hands on my balls and offers me sex for $250. I tell her I'm from Belfast. She doesn't know where it is, so I say London instead. Ulga's been to London, once, on holiday with a man. She liked Piccadilly Circus, she says, squeezing my balls tighter. It is not easy to get away, but I do.

Towards dawn I talk to Gloria, the bartender. She is stunning, more so than any of the prostitutes. Like Ula, she studies at the state university, and hates her job. Unlike Ula, she doesn't earn at least $1000 a month, she earns more like $250. But it's worth it. She doesn't get to be groped by greasy businessmen, and one day she will have saved up enough to go to Paris.

I leave Night Flight disappointed not to have got any pictures. But on my way home I capture two prostitutes sleeping on a park bench which perhaps says more than my whole evening in the club.

Furniture

A fortnight ago I gave Igor $200 for four weeks' keep. With this money, he's started to buy a whole heap of old furniture which he's hoping to be able to sell. It seems a good plan, but I do worry. Our flat is turning into an antique shop. In every room there's a surplus wardrobe, table, or chair. It's impossible to move about the place. Igor hasn't yet managed to sell one piece, and has already blown nearly all the money.

The furniture itself is crumbling. I remind Igor that people might be reluctant to pay good money for a table with only three legs. He insists he can repair it, but never does. In an effort to get rid of it all, Igor has placed several advertisements in newspapers, and plastered every available lamp-post with his own homemade ads.

Homemade ads, much used by Muscovites, are ingenious and ubiquitous. I first saw Sasha making them. They are made of a piece of paper, on which the ad is written along the top. At the bottom a small fringe is cut, so the paper resembles one of those old-fashioned book-marks. The advertiser's telephone number is written on every frond, each of which is detachable. This means that those interested in what's on offer, who are as likely as not standing in heavy snow, don't have to freeze while fumbling for a pen and notebook.

Today a woman responds to one of the hundreds of homemade ads with which Igor seems to have decorated the whole of Moscow. She wants the wardrobe. We have huge problems fitting it into the lift, but eventually manage to get it out of the building.

In the evening he returns bearing a bottle of champagne to celebrate his first sale. I ask if he's made a profit. Only a small one, he says. The old woman didn't have much money. Igor took pity on her, and couldn't bring himself even to demand the asking price.

Communist demonstration

'Yeltsin is a whore', 'Yeltsin has destroyed the great Russia', 'Yeltsin has ruined our army'.

About 25,000 Communist demonstrators, mostly of the older generation, are shouting as they make their way to Manezh Square. Red Square, with Lenin's tomb, is their preferred destination, but the government has closed it off to them. The angry crowd is marching in defence of Fatherland Day (formerly known as Soviet Army and Navy Day), and to attack Boris Yeltsin's policies. It is one of the largest demonstrations since the collapse of Soviet Russia.

I photograph from a truck filled with Communist supporters. As it moves through the crowd, the scene in front of me is spectacular. Hundreds of the old red flags, and the gold and black banners of the Liberal Democratic Party, brighten the all pervading greyness.

In the midst of all this, everyday life can be glimpsed on the pavements, carrying on as if nothing's happening. One couple is struggling with their tiresome toddler. A woman is trying to sell a painting. People are queueing for a bus. They're in for a long wait.

When the demonstration reaches Manezh Square itself, it is already dark. There is a minute's silence in memory of those who died in war. A middle-aged woman, desperately moved, is trying to hold back the tears. It is as if she is mourning, also, the loss of an empire.

Kifir/tuna fish

For two weeks now Igor and I have lived solely on a diet of kifir and bread, with the occasional Snickers bar thrown in. Kifir is unbearably sour and gritty. It becomes a meal when mixed with a dried yogurt which comes in a block like butter. Combined they look like cottage cheese, but much less appetizing.

Kifir is a health food, often doled out to sick children and is good for intestinal problems. This is how I first discovered it, but we continue to eat the kifir because there's fuck all else. Unlike almost everything, it isn't in short supply. It's also very cheap. Igor swears by it and can't eat enough of the stuff. For me, it's a constant struggle.

Yesterday we graduated to tuna fish which, in comparison to kifir, was like Harrods' smoked salmon. We had the tuna with rice and onion, having found it in a kiosk close to the flat. The kiosk also sold Spar ravioli – bliss in a tin. When we served the meal up we became tense and touchy. Igor counted my ravioli pieces to make sure I hadn't cheated. We ate at a snail's pace, wanting to relish every mouthful. The taste was so good.

Unfortunately, these luxuries no longer exist. Today, the kiosk owner tells us he only got them by chance. We are now back on the kifir. If we are what we eat, I am exceptionally gritty and sour.

Gorbachev

5 March 1993 – Mikhail Gorbachev is giving a short talk to about sixty western businessmen in the American Business Centre, Moscow.

At the table nobody is talking to him. I am sitting three feet from him. Lunch is about to start. It looks delicious – chicken, sauté potatoes – one of the best looking meals I've seen since arriving. I am more excited at the prospect of eating this than I am at hearing Gorbachev speak live. Just as the food is about to be served, he turns to me and says, 'Bon appetit.' I stumble for words, and don't manage to say much.

When we finish eating, Gorbachev makes a rambling speech about the political situation in Russia, after which there are questions.

'Political analysts here and around the world,' begins a journalist, 'are saying President Yeltsin has lost most of his power. Even allies of Yeltsin's recently said, "Yeltsin is as powerless as the Queen of England". Do you agree?'

Gorbachev replies, 'I would like to answer the first part of that question, and I will drop the rest because I'm not in a jokey mood.

'In answering the first part of the question, I wouldn't reduce all the things that are happening today to just one personality. I'd like to draw our attention to the fact that, today, we should make a clear assessment of the policies that were pursued since the beginning of 1992. Without such analysis we will not arrive at the choices we have to make today and tomorrow, and in this connection the consequences of such a policy, and where we stand now.

News brief

This is how we should assess the role played by President Yeltsin and the Russian government.'

Yeltsin Warns, Then Walks

President Boris Yeltsin warned law-makers that if they did not remove power-limiting measures from a draft resolution, 'I shall really be forced to think about additional measures to preserve the balance of powers in the country.' When the Congress refused to change the resolution, he walked out of the chamber along with top aides and members of his cabinet.

Congress Passes Resolution

After Yeltsin left, Congress voted 656–184 with 41 abstentions to approve the resolution that stripped him of his executive powers. The measure gives the law-makers the right to veto Yeltsin's decrees and returns to the cabinet the power to introduce legislation, further diminishing presidential authority. It also cancels an agreement to hold an 11 April referendum.

The Moscow Times, 13 March 1993

News Briefs

What the people say

Sidewalk Survey:
Does the Congress Affect You?

Olga Manicheva, 35, developer
No, they won't make any difference to me. I don't really believe that Yeltsin will fall, but I hope he doesn't, because I want things to stay as they are, and I would rather have a Pinochet than a Stalin. I think Khasbulatov is like Stalin. And I don't really think it would be dangerous for Yeltsin to have more power.

Alexander Leskis, 46, unemployed
Yes, I think the Congress affects me personally. Sooner or later, there will have to be a referendum. Even the deputies see that. But I am worried that Yeltsin will be forced out. I want to see Russia become a presidential republic, and I think Yeltsin is necessary to the survival of the country. All this is just a pointless struggle.

Olga Chernikova, 20, student
I don't think this Congress really affects me. I know there will be a referendum and I think I would like a presidential republic. I think that would give the country more order. But it's all so complicated. I do think it would be dangerous if Yeltsin fell from power, because then we'd have to get used to someone new all over again.

Boris Golovichev, 35, engineer
The Congress is important to me, but not very important. It's a pathetic Congress. I don't think the Congress will change anything at all. I doubt anything good will come of it. It certainly won't be any better. We might get a different leader, and I don't think we'd get a worse one. I support reforms, but not Yeltsin.

Alevtina Slusayeva, 60, pensioner
All they are doing at that Congress is arguing, and not producing anything. We need someone with the power of Stalin – not that I think Stalin was good, you understand – but it was good that there was someone who could take control of the country. Now we have no strong leader. Now we have nothing.

The Moscow Times, 13 March 1993

Support for Yeltsin

All day I've been hanging around outside the Kremlin. Things are heated in there at the moment, and I'm convinced anything might happen. Yesterday, when Yeltsin walked out of Congress, rumours of tanks in Red Square started to abound. The 'tanks' turned out to be snow ploughs.

The city centre is hauntingly quiet, and there's tension in the air. People can only speculate about what's actually going on. As I start my fourth Snickers bar of the day, I spy thousands of people being led by military men down Teatralnaya. They've suddenly appeared, out of the blue, and taken me completely by surprise.

They are of all ages, out to support Yeltsin in his hour of need. Congress has been giving him a lot of grief these past forty-eight hours. They have stripped him of most of his powers, and cancelled the 11 April referendum.

Many bystanders are moved spontaneously to join in their march. When they arrive outside the Kremlin, they find a crowd of 8000 hardliners have beaten them to it. It's so bizarre to see both sides unintentionally happen upon each other, it's almost funny. Even the policemen giggle.

The number of Yeltsin supporters far outweighs that of the hardliners. If this is anything to go by, and there is a referendum, it seems obvious what the result will be.

Soon enough we learn that the outcome of Yeltsin's ultimatum to Congress is a compromise. Yeltsin won't be stripped of all his powers, and the referendum's not been cancelled, but postponed, till 25 April.

Igor plans to move to the centre

This morning Igor asks me to lend him 2000 roubles. This evening he returns with three pots of white paint. I learn it is for his new flat in the centre of Moscow. He wants to be there because it's so much livelier, and he's had enough of the wretched buses.

Apparently there's an old woman living in a large flat close to Arbat Street. According to him she's 'about to die'. He intends to be the first to move in when she does.

Has he met her? I ask.

Yes.

Does she know he plans to stage a coup?

No. But he's going to start negotiating with her soon.

London, May 1993

When I speak to Igor on the phone this evening, he tells me the woman's not yet dead but, unable to wait any longer, he's moving in with her next week.

Oh, so you're her toy-boy, now, are you? I ask.

No, I am informed sharply. He's her rent-free home-help.

Decide to leave Moscow

I've decided to leave Moscow because I'm now totally skint. Igor has been completely sweet, and offered me his last $10, but I can't accept it.

I ring my bank manager in Belfast to ask if he'll extend my overdraft 'just a little'.

'No chance,' he says, and gives me a lot of grief for already being over the limit.

My bank manager drives a very big sports car – he's obviously compensating for deficiencies elsewhere.

Reserving ticket and leaving

At Moscow station, I queue for over an hour at the one and only international train ticket desk in the entire city. All I need to do is check the timetable. When I finally make it to the counter, I learn I need a seat reservation ticket which costs $30, as well as the return ticket I bought in London months ago. I am livid. All I have is one copeck in my pocket. Where on earth am I going to get $30 in the short time before my train is due to leave?

Igor and I search our brains for a solution. I hit upon the idea of selling my Walkman. There are no headphones and it doesn't work properly but the motor still turns, so when I demonstrate it to a potential buyer he or she may still just be fooled. I'm in with a chance.

We spot a gaggle of Mafia types near a kiosk. Igor holds our place in the queue at the international desk while I approach the group. I emphasize to these dangerous figures that the Walkman's an Aiwa, that it's top quality, state-of-the-art, and that with headphones it sounds really great. One offers me $10 for it. I have to refuse.

I walk away. Now I have only minutes till the train departs. Desperate, I go up to a smart-looking man who turns out to be Austrian. I'm extremely polite to him as I relate my plight. My story, being genuine, obviously moves him, for he hands me $20.

'Thank you very much,' I say. 'I'd do the same for you.'

I'm still $10 short, so return, running, to the Mafia guys and tell them they can have the Walkman for what they offered after all. Their interest has dimmed. I do everything in my power to whip it up again. The minutes are ticking by.

Just when I'm giving up hope, another Mafia guy appears and readily stumps up the cash. I sprint back to Igor, get the miserable reservation ticket, astounding the salesgirl in the process. She congratulates me on my enterprise.

Igor and I run to the platform. Before I get on the train, I take off my Doc Marten boots and hand them to him. He's always coveted them. We hug, no words. I get on the train, wondering when I'll see him again.

As the train pulls away, I look out of the window. The Mafia man is running after the train, shaking the Walkman in his fist, shouting at me, and trying to catch up with my carriage. As he does so, Igor wobbles past him, unaware of the drama. His back is to me, but I can see that in one hand he is clutching his DMs, and with the other he's scratching his leg. His bugs are obviously still bothering him.

Home

After living in Moscow for some months, I'm now back in Belfast, back to bombs, back to bank managers, and back to boredom. I weigh a spectacularly low eight and a quarter stone (I'm six foot), and the doctor has put me on a diet of scrambled eggs, and more 'Build-ups' milk protein drinks.

Despite all this, I am transported by the mundane details of life which, since my trip, have become all-important pleasures. The smell of fresh vegetables; a sizzling steak; the convenience of the coffee maker, the microwave, the toaster – all of these I used to take so much for granted I didn't even notice them. Now they fill me with untold delight. I am like a child discovering new joys.

Belfast is warm. I'm walking around in a light shirt, and can feel my body against the air again. Marvellous. I travel on buses, and my face isn't pressed up against a frozen window, or a hostile chest. People aren't shouting at me in the street for no apparent reason. Supermarket shelves are so full and colourful I am dizzied, and the queues at the efficient check-outs are short and fast. (I never thought *that* before!) When I want to call a friend, I get through, and I'm not cut off mid-conversation. I can walk into my own home without risking a night in a dodgy lift. Once there, I can use a toilet which doesn't sway when I sit on it, and loo-paper feels like velvet.

Hospital

I've been home just a week and now I find myself writing from a hospital bed. Moscow screwed up my digestive system, and I was rushed in here with an appendix grumbling so much it was fit to burst. The nurses are very worried about me. They give me more baths a day than I used to have in Russia in a month and, in an effort to fatten me up, they supplement the hospital food with delicious supplies of their own.

My doctor jokes how lucky I am: had the grumble started in Moscow, the surgeon would have plied me with vodka and whipped the appendix out just like that. I wince at the thought.

Missing Moscow

My hospital sojourn did not last long. Shortage of beds meant the NHS couldn't keep me so I'm convalescing at home. It's three minutes to midnight. I try to ring Igor. Today on the radio, I heard that thousands of Muscovites were in Red Square demonstrating for Yeltsin. No doubt Igor was there amongst them. I wish that I had been too.